W9-BUB-330

My First
SCIENCE
Dictionary

My First SCIENCE Dictionary

By Sarah Rabkin

**Illustrated by
Dianne O'Quinn Burke**

CHECKERBOARD PRESS

NEW YORK

For my parents
—S. R.

For the preservation of our beautiful planet
and all the living things on it.
—D. O. B.

Acknowledgments

Several scientists reviewed the dictionary in manuscript form; their expert critiques helped ensure the book's thoroughness and accuracy. Thanks go to the following people:

Stephen F. Bailey, Ph.D., Collections Manager, Department of Ornithology and Mammology, California Academy of Sciences, San Francisco (*biology*)

Jean F. DeMouthe, Ph.D., Senior Collections Manager, Department of Invertebrate Zoology and Geology, California Academy of Sciences, San Francisco (*geology*)

Mycol Doyle, Ph.D., Adjunct Professor of Biology, California Polytechnic University, San Luis Obispo, California (*botany*)

Brian Harris, Ph.D., President, Lorquin Entomological Society, and Curator of Entomology, Natural History Museum of Los Angeles (*biology*)

Jonathon Hodge, Planetarium Director, Santa Monica College, Santa Monica, California (*astronomy*)

William Pearce, Ph.D., Associate Professor of Physiology, Loma Linda University School of Medicine, Loma Linda, California (*physiology and biology*)

Andrew Smith, Ph.D., Department Manager of Superconductive Electronics Research, Space and Technology Group, TRW, Redondo Beach, California (*physics*)

In addition, Larry Pageler applied a scientist's precision, an eagle editorial eye, and a vivid memory of his own childhood fascination with science to his readings of early drafts, and contributed valuable suggestions and corrections at every stage. Finally, Lisa Melton, the dictionary's editor at RGA Publishing Group, provided careful editing and limitless enthusiasm for the project. She deserves much of the credit for its successful completion.

—S. R.

Copyright © 1992 RGA Publishing Group, Inc. All rights reserved.
ISBN: 1-56288-215-5

Printed in U.S.A.   0   9   8   7   6   5   4   3   2   1

Published by Checkerboard Press, Inc.
30 Vesey Street, New York, NY 10007

Note to Parents, Teachers, and Friends

The toughest challenge in creating a young children's science dictionary is deciding what not to include. Science is a broad subject, encompassing thousands of words that are likely to interest young children. In order to assemble a useful, inviting, and instructive dictionary of manageable size, the author and editors have consulted school curriculum writers, parents, and educators, designing a word list with the following criteria in mind:

1. The words must be those that children are likely to encounter in the course of their daily lives at home and/or at school;

2. The words can be defined quickly, simply, and accurately, in terms that children can understand; and

3. Each word must represent a fundamental concept in science, an aspect of a scientific issue with contemporary significance, or an interesting scientific fact likely to excite children.

The resulting word list is balanced among a variety of subject categories within the physical and life sciences, including the following: the earth; the human body; light and atmosphere; matter, force, and physical phenomena; plants, animals, and nature; space and astronomy; weather and temperature; and the practice of science. Some categories of applied science, such as health and medicine as well as machines and technology, have been purposely omitted in order to maintain a reasonable focus.

We suggest that you keep the dictionary handy, to be consulted whenever a child asks you the meaning of a science-related word during conversation or while you are reading aloud. By encouraging children to use this book, you can help promote and satisfy their curiosity about how the world works. You can also help them acquire the powers of independent learning that come with knowing how to use a reference book. Children who can read on their own but who have little experience with dictionaries may find it helpful to work through the following introduction with you before looking up words by themselves.

Introduction for Kids: How to Use This Dictionary

A dictionary tells you at least two things about a word: the meaning, or **definition**, of the word, and the correct **spelling** of the word. This book is a science dictionary, so it tells you about words that have to do with science.

Take a look at the definition of **science** below.

entry word (spelling) *phonetic spelling* *part of speech* *definition*

science (SY-unss) *noun*

Science is the study of the universe, everything in it, and how it all works. Science has many different branches. Biology, geology, astronomy, and chemistry are all branches of science.

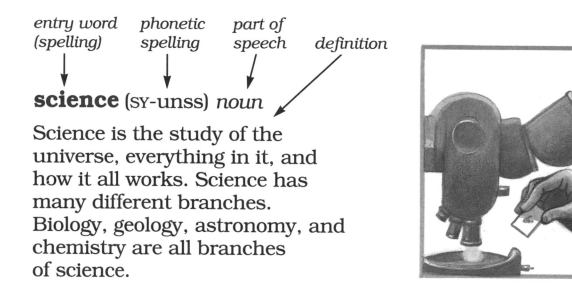

You'll see that, in addition to being defined, the **entry word** is also spelled out phonetically. This **phonetic spelling** tells you how to sound out the word **science**. Note that the first syllable, SY, is capitalized. This is the syllable you should **stress** when pronouncing the word. (The **pronunciation key** at the front of this book will help you learn how to read the phonetic spellings in this dictionary.)

After the phonetic spelling, you'll find the name of the kind of word you're looking at—a noun, a verb, or an adjective. These are different **parts of speech**. Nouns are names of things. Verbs are actions. And adjectives describe things.

In addition to being defined, some of the words in **MY FIRST SCIENCE DICTIONARY** also come with extra information and interesting facts. Look for these on the same page as the definition.

How do you look up words in a dictionary? Say you want to know the meaning of the word **dinosaur**. What should you do? Look it up in the dictionary, of course. But like most dictionaries, this one has many pages. It could take you a long time to look through the book page by page until you found the right word.

Fortunately, there is an easier way. The words in a dictionary are always arranged **alphabetically** (in the order of the alphabet) so that you can find them quickly. This means that all the words beginning with the letter **a** are grouped together, and come before all the words that begin with the letter **b**, which come before all the words that begin with the letter **c**, and so on through the letter **z**.

Now let's begin our search. **Dinosaur** begins with the letter **d**, so it would be in the part of the dictionary with all the other **d** words. Since **d** is towards the beginning of the alphabet, we would expect to find **dinosaur** somewhere near the beginning of the book.

When you find the words beginning with **d**, you will notice that there are quite a few of them. How do you know where exactly to find **dinosaur**? Look at the first few words that begin with **d**:

decompose   **desert**   **digestion**   **dinosaur**

Why are these words ordered the way they are? When first letters match (in this case **d**), we look at the *second letter*. But both **decompose** and **desert** have **e** as a second letter, so what do we do? We look at the *third letter*. **Desert** comes after **decompose** because **s** comes after **c** in the alphabet. We also know that **desert** comes before **digestion**, because, looking at the second letter of each word, **e** comes before **i**. Finally, we come upon **dinosaur**, which follows **digestion** because, even though both words begin with **di**, **g** comes before **n** in the alphabet.

Which would you find first in the dictionary, **continent** or **constellation**? If you chose **constellation** you'd be right. The first three letters of these two words match, but the fourth letter of **constellation** comes before the fourth letter of **continent**. You can see how easy it is to look up words in a dictionary!

Keep **MY FIRST SCIENCE DICTIONARY** handy whenever you are reading, listening to someone read, or just talking. If you come upon a word you don't quite understand, practice looking it up. And if you want to know the meaning of a word that isn't in this book, ask an adult to help you look for the word in a dictionary for older people!

Aa

air (AYR) noun

Air is the invisible mixture of gases that surrounds the Earth. Most animals, plants, and other living things need air to stay alive.

altitude (AL-tih-tood) noun

Altitude tells you how high something is above the surface of the sea. If a town is 100 feet above sea level, then we say it has an altitude of 100 feet. Sometimes altitude means height above the ground instead of height above the sea.

Where's the highest place in North America? The lowest?

The highest altitude in North America is in the state of Alaska, at the top of Mount McKinley. The lowest altitude on land in North America (and in all the Americas) is in the state of California, in Death Valley National Monument.

Mount McKinley
20,320 feet
above sea level

Death Valley
282 feet
below sea level

amphibian

(am-FIB-ee-un) *noun*

An amphibian is a kind of back-boned animal that, typically, spends its early life in water, breathing through gills. Then it develops lungs to breathe air and lives on land. Female amphibians lay eggs. Frogs, toads, newts, and salamanders are all amphibians.

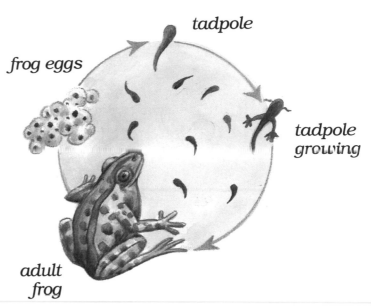

frog eggs

tadpole

tadpole growing

adult frog

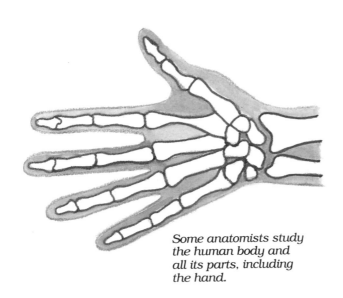

Some anatomists study the human body and all its parts, including the hand.

anatomy

(uh-NAT-uh-mee) *noun*

Anatomy is the science of bodies—the bodies of humans and other animals, and of plants, fungi, and other life-forms, too. People who study anatomy are called anatomists. They look at all the different parts of bodies, as well as how those body parts work together.

artery (AR-ter-ee) *noun*

Arteries are the long, flexible tubes (also called blood vessels) that carry blood toward all parts of the body from the heart. If you lay your fingers firmly over the inside of your wrist, you may be able to feel your blood pulsing through the arteries that lie under the skin. Blood pulses through the arteries each time it is pumped by the heart.

asteroid (AS-tuh-royd) *noun*

An asteroid is a very small, rocky planet orbiting the Sun. Our solar system contains thousands of asteroids, and most of them lie between the orbits of Mars and Jupiter.

astronomy
(uh-STRON-uh-mee) *noun*

Astronomy is the study of stars, planets, moons, galaxies, and all the other objects in the universe beyond the Earth. People who work in the field of astronomy are called astronomers. They use telescopes and other tools to find out how large objects in space are, how they move, what they are made of, how far away they are from the Earth, and more.

atmosphere
(AT-muh-sfeer) *noun*

The atmosphere is the blanket of air and moisture that surrounds the Earth. It is made up mostly of nitrogen and oxygen. From space, Earth's atmosphere looks blue and white. Other planets have atmospheres that are different from ours.

Moon

Earth

atom (AT-um) *noun*

An atom is a very small particle that is so tiny that you can't see it, smell it, or feel it. All objects are made of atoms. There are many kinds of atoms, and they are all made up of even smaller parts. The three main parts of atoms are called protons, neutrons, and electrons.

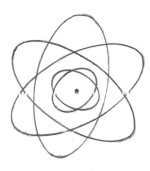

avalanche
(AV-uh-lanch) *noun*

An avalanche is a huge pile of snow, ice, and rocks falling down a slope such as a mountainside. Avalanches may carry dirt and trees with them. Very loud noises, or the footsteps of people tramping by, can cause an avalanche. So can rain or the hot sunshine melting snow.

Bb

bacterium (bak-TEER-ee-um) *noun*
plural: bacteria (bak-TEER-ee-uh)

Bacteria are tiny living things made of only one cell. They are among the simplest forms of life on our planet. Even though bacteria are too small to see, they are just about everywhere. Some bacteria cause sickness or tooth decay. Other bacteria are used to make medicine (such as some antibiotics) or foods (such as cheese and yogurt).

magnified Diplocci bacteria

13

bay (BAY) *noun*

A bay is a small body of water attached to a bigger body of water, such as an ocean or a big lake. Some bays, like San Francisco Bay, have cities on their shores.

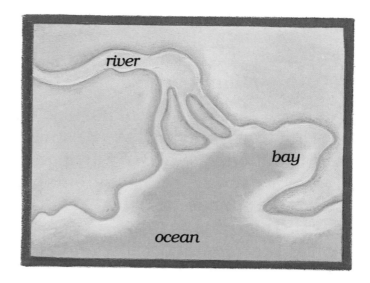

plant

fungus

animal

biology (by-OL-oh-jee) *noun*

Biology is the study of life. People who work in the field of biology are called biologists. Some biologists work outdoors, observing plants, animals, and other forms of life. Other biologists do experiments in laboratories. Some do both.

bird (BERD) *noun*

A bird is a feather-covered animal that has two legs and two wings. Female birds lay eggs. Most birds can fly, but some, like penguins and ostriches, cannot. Robins, sea gulls, chickens, and eagles are all birds.

robin

black hole (BLAK HOHL) *noun*

A black hole is a place in outer space where gravity is so strong that nothing can escape. Not even light can escape a black hole—that is why it is black. A black hole forms when a huge star collapses into a very small, dense ball.

moose

blizzard (BLIZ-erd) *noun*

A blizzard is a very strong snowstorm, with fast winds, blinding thick snow, and freezing air.

blood (BLUD) *noun*

Blood is the red fluid that moves through the small tubes in your body called blood vessels. Blood brings food and oxygen to all parts of your body and carries away waste. It contains red blood cells, which carry oxygen, and white blood cells, which help your body fight disease.

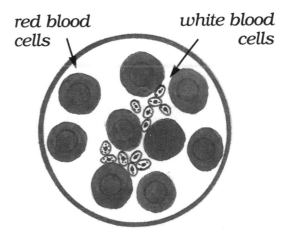

red blood cells

white blood cells

boil (BOYL) verb

To boil a liquid means to heat the liquid until it bubbles and becomes a gas. Water boils at 212 degrees Fahrenheit—far too hot to touch. Some liquids, such as cooking oil, boil when they are even hotter. Other liquids, such as liquid nitrogen, boil when they are much colder than ice.

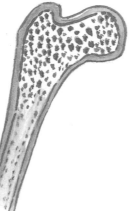

inside view of your thighbone

bone (BOHN) noun

Bones are the hard, strong parts of your body that make up your skeleton. Some bones, like your backbone, help you to stand and move. Other bones, such as your ribs, protect the soft parts of your body. Bones are made mainly of the mineral calcium, which makes them hard. You have more than 200 bones in your body.

brain (BRAYN) noun

The brain is the large grayish-white organ inside your skull. It is the part of your body that thinks, learns, and understands. It is like the body's computer, sending messages to the rest of your body so you can see, hear, smell, move, balance, talk, feel, and create.

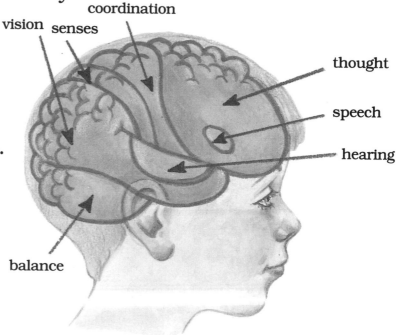

various centers in the brain

butterfly (BUT-er-fly) *noun*

A butterfly is a kind of insect that has two pairs of large, flat, often colorful wings that work together as a single pair. The wings are covered with tiny hairs or scales. Butterflies usually feed and fly during the day.

tiger swallowtail

How does a caterpillar become a butterfly?

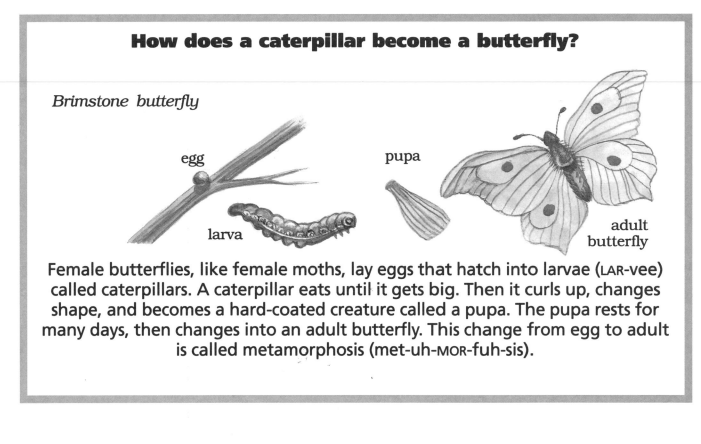

Brimstone butterfly

egg

larva

pupa

adult butterfly

Female butterflies, like female moths, lay eggs that hatch into larvae (LAR-vee) called caterpillars. A caterpillar eats until it gets big. Then it curls up, changes shape, and becomes a hard-coated creature called a pupa. The pupa rests for many days, then changes into an adult butterfly. This change from egg to adult is called metamorphosis (met-uh-MOR-fuh-sis).

Cc

carbon dioxide (KAR-bon dy-OKSS-eyed) *noun*

Carbon dioxide is one of the gases in the Earth's atmosphere. While plants use carbon dioxide to make food, humans and many other animals exhale it as waste when they breathe. You cannot see carbon dioxide.

caterpillar (KAT-ur-pil-ur) *noun*

A caterpillar is the larva of a butterfly or moth. It looks somewhat like a fat worm, but it has three pairs of real legs and many false legs. Some caterpillars are very colorful.

Clanothus California silk-moth

cell (SELL) *noun*

A cell is a tiny unit of life. All living things (except viruses) are made of cells. Most cells contain many different smaller units, each of which has a special job to do. The smallest organisms are made of just one cell. Your body is made up of more than 50,000,000,000,000 (fifty trillion) cells!

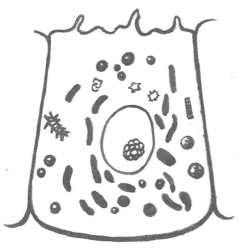

chemistry (KEM-uh-stree) *noun*

Chemistry is the science of what things are made of, how they combine with each other, and how they change. People who work in the field of chemistry are called chemists.

18

climate (KLY-mut) noun

The climate of a place is the kind of weather that that place has over a long period of time. Southern California has a mostly sunny climate all year long. Chicago has a cold winter climate and a warm summer climate.

cloud (KLOWD) noun

A cloud is a large clump of tiny water droplets or bits of ice in the air. Clouds are white or gray, but during sunrise or sunset, the sunlight can make them look different colors. Some clouds drop rain, hail, or snow on the ground. There are three main kinds of clouds.

cumulus   *cirrus*   *stratus*

cold-blooded (KOLD-BLUD-ed) adjective

Cold-blooded animals are animals whose body temperatures change with the temperature of the surrounding area. Reptiles, amphibians, and fish are all cold-blooded.

marine iguana

19

comet (KOM-et) *noun*

A comet is a large ball of frozen gas and dust in space. Comets orbit the Sun. When a comet nears the Sun it develops a long, glowing tail that can be seen in the night sky. Some comet tails can be millions of miles long.

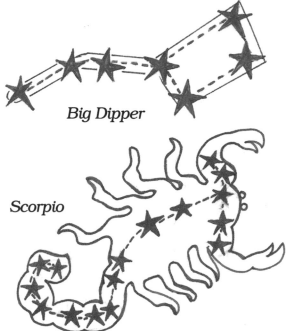

Big Dipper

Scorpio

constellation
(kon-stuh-LAY-shun) *noun*

A constellation is a group of stars in the sky. Many constellations were named after something they look like. The constellation Scorpio looks like a scorpion. The Big Dipper looks like a dipper, or ladle.

continent
(KON-tih-nent) *noun*

A continent is a huge piece of land. There are seven continents on the Earth: Africa, Antarctica, Asia, Australia, Europe, North America, and South America. Sometimes people group Asia and Europe together and call them Eurasia.

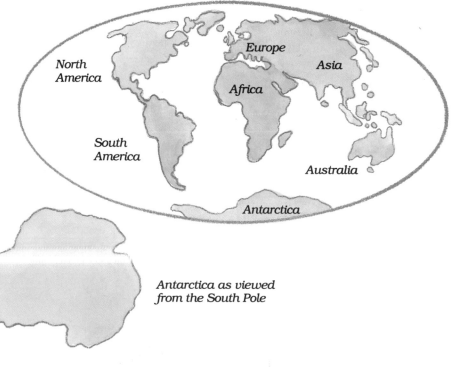

Antarctica as viewed from the South Pole

crater (KRAYT-ur) noun

A crater is a bowl-shaped hole in the ground. Some craters are miles across, while others are just a few feet wide. Craters can be created when a volcano erupts, or when a meteoroid from space crashes to the Earth. The Moon is covered with craters made by meteoroids.

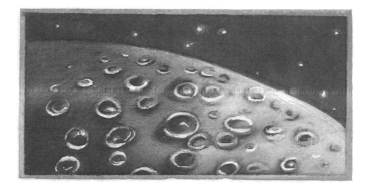

Dd

decompose
(dee-kum-POHZ) verb

To decompose is to break down into smaller parts, or to rot. Old, crumbling, weather-beaten rocks are decomposing. A brown apple core in your lunchbox and a moldy leaf in the woods are also decomposing. Bacteria, fungi, and other tiny life-forms help dead things to decompose.

desert (DEZ-ert) noun

A desert is a very dry place that is usually rocky or sandy and has no trees. Only special kinds of animals and plants can survive in the desert. Two of the world's great deserts are the Sahara in Africa and the Gobi in Asia. The continent of Antarctica is also a desert!

cactus

king snake

crested dragon

side-blotched lizard

digestion (dy-JESS-chun) *noun*

Digestion is the process by which your body breaks down food to give you energy and to build your body. Your teeth, tongue, stomach, intestines, liver, and other organs help with digestion.

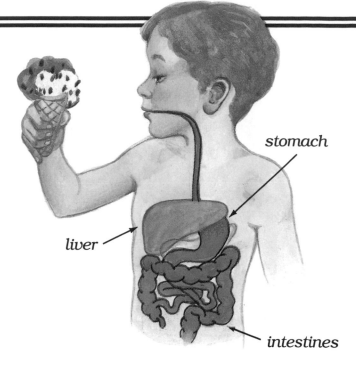

stomach

liver

intestines

Apatosaurus

dinosaur (DY-nuh-sor) *noun*

Dinosaurs were reptiles that once lived on the Earth. There were meat-eating dinosaurs and plant-eating ones. One type of dinosaur evolved into birds. Dinosaurs became extinct about 65 million years ago. Scientists have different ideas as to how that happened.

How big were the dinosaurs?

Stegosaurus

Tyrannosaurus rex

There were many kinds of dinosaurs, and they came in many shapes and sizes. Some were as small as chickens. Others were huge—as big as twenty of you lying head-to-toe on the ground in one long line.

drought (DROWT) *noun*

A drought is a time of extra-dry weather. In a drought, rain doesn't fall as often as usual. The soil dries out, plants die, and sometimes people and animals do not have enough water to survive.

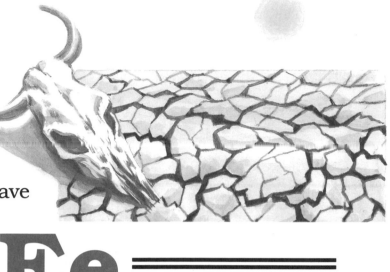

Ee

Earth (ERTH) *noun*

The Earth is a roundish ball in space, made mostly of rock. It is the third planet from the Sun. It is the planet we live on and the only planet we know of where life exists. Most of the Earth's surface is covered with water. The word "earth" is also used to mean soil, dirt, land, or ground.

A look inside the Earth

The Earth is made up of three different layers. The part you stand on, the crust, is made of rock and is about 25 miles deep. This seems thick to us, but compared to the rest of the Earth it is like the skin on an apple. Under the crust is a thicker layer of different rock, called the mantle. The innermost layer, made mostly of nickel and iron, is called the core.

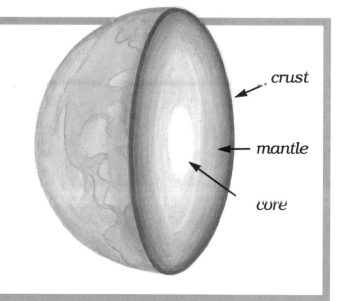

crust

mantle

core

earthquake (ERTH-kwayk) *noun*

An earthquake is a trembling of the ground. Some earthquakes shake the ground so gently that you can't even feel them. Some are so strong that they destroy buildings.

What makes the ground quake?

The Earth's crust is split into several pieces, or plates. These plates are always slowly moving past each other—so slowly that we do not usually notice. However, sometimes one piece of the crust gets stuck and cannot move past another piece. It pushes until it finally breaks free. This sudden breaking free makes ground shake in an earthquake.

A place where the Earth's crust is split apart is called a fault.

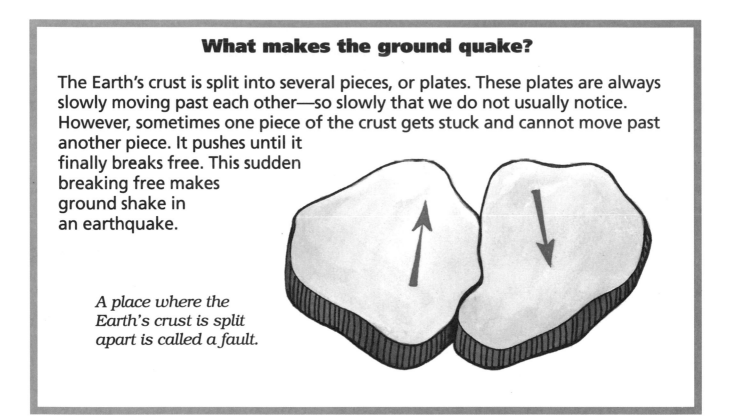

eclipse (ih-KLIPSS) *noun*

An eclipse is a blocking of the Sun's light by the Earth or the Moon. In a lunar eclipse, the Earth moves between the Sun and the full Moon, blocking the sunlight so that the Moon is in shadow and appears dark for a little while. In a solar eclipse, the Moon moves between the Sun and the Earth, blocking our view of the Sun.

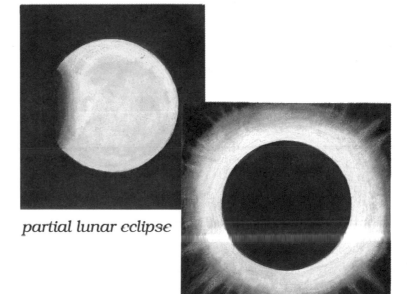

partial lunar eclipse

total solar eclipse

24

ecology (ih-KOL-uh-jee) noun

Ecology is the study of how plants, animals, and other living things live with each other and with their environment. People who work in the field of ecology are called ecologists.

plants and animals of the tide pool environment

cheetah

kit fox

grizzly bear

endangered
(in-DAYN-jurd) adjective

Endangered means "in danger." Endangered species are animals, plants, and other life-forms that are in danger of becoming extinct.

Saguaro cactus

environment (in-VY-run-ment) noun

Environment means "surroundings." The environment of a place, person, plant, or animal includes all the things and conditions (like climate) that surround and affect them. There are many kinds of environments: mountains, deserts, and rain forests are just a few. When people talk about "the environment," they usually mean everything that surrounds and affects all the living things on Earth.

25

erosion (ih-ROH-zhun) *noun*

Erosion is the wearing away of the Earth's surface. Wind, water, heating, cooling, and glaciers cause erosion by blowing, washing, cracking, and scraping the rock and soil away. Where plants grow, erosion is slowed down.

evaporate (ih-VAP-uh-rayt) *verb*

When a liquid evaporates, it turns into a gas and escapes into the air. If you leave a dish of water outside on a hot, dry day, the water will evaporate slowly. After a few days or maybe even a few hours, the dish will be dry.

evolution (ev-uh-LOO-shun) *noun*

Evolution is the process by which living things change over time. Life began on Earth billions of years ago, but back then it didn't look anything like it does today. Over the years, some organisms have become extinct, and others have evolved —passed new looks and new ways of living on to their children and grandchildren.

the evolution of humans

Australo-pithecus

Homo habilis

Neanderthal

Homo sapien

experiment
(ik-SPAIR-uh-ment) *noun, verb*

An experiment is a test to discover something or to see how something works. When you put a dish of water outside to see how long it will take to evaporate, you are performing an experiment. "Experiment" is also the word for *doing* tests. Try experimenting with evaporation!

Pterosaur

dodo bird

extinct (ik-STINKT) *adjective*

A group of animals or plants is extinct if the whole group has died out. The Pterosaur and dodo bird are two kinds of extinct animals.

Ff

fish (FISH) *noun*

A fish is a backboned animal that lives only in the water and usually has fins but no legs or arms. Fish have gills instead of lungs for breathing. Most fishes' bodies are covered with tiny hard plates called scales. Most female fish lay eggs in the water, but some give birth to living young. Goldfish, tuna, and sharks are all fish, but whales and dolphins are not.

goldfish

27

fog (FOG) *noun*

Fog is a cloud that is very close to the ground or to the surface of the ocean. Sometimes fog can be very thick, making it difficult to see an object just a few feet away from you!

force (FORSS) *noun*

A force is a push or a pull. When you catch a big fish, the force of the fish pulls on the line. When you push the pedals on a bicycle with your feet, you are using the force of your muscles to move the bicycle.

fossil (FOSS-ul) *noun*

A fossil is a leftover part or print of a plant or animal that lived a long time ago. A fossil can be a footprint, an imprint of a shell or a plant, a bone, or even a whole animal that was preserved for many years in rock, hardened tree sap, or ice.

fossil of an oak leaf

friction (FRIK-shun) *noun*

Friction is one object rubbing against another. Without friction, all things would slide past each other without sticking. When you rub your palms together fast, friction causes them to heat up.

an orange protects seeds

fruit (FROOT) *noun*

A fruit is the part of a flowering plant that contains and protects the plant's seeds. Fruits come in many sizes, shapes, textures, and flavors. They can be hard or soft, dry or fleshy, dull or colorful, sweet or sour, healthful or poisonous. Oranges and apples are fruits. So are tomatoes and pumpkins!

fungus (FUN-guss) *noun*
plural: fungi (FUN-jy)

A fungus is a plantlike organism that cannot make its own food the way a green plant does. Instead, it gets its energy by decomposing living or dead plants and animals. Fungi have no leaves, flowers, or seeds. Mushrooms, toadstools, truffles, mildews, molds, and yeast are all fungi.

gill fungus mycena

29

Gg

galaxy (GAL-uk-see) *noun*

A galaxy is a huge group of stars, planets, gas, and dust that is held together by gravity and surrounded by empty space. Some galaxies are shaped like spheres or ovals, and others have stranger shapes. Our planet, the Earth, is in a spiral-shaped galaxy that we call the Milky Way.

spiral galaxy

Steam is a gas.

gas (GASS) *noun*

Gas is a light, shapeless vapor. It is one of the three states, or forms, that matter comes in. (The other two forms are solid and liquid.) There are many kinds of gas. The oxygen that an underwater diver carries in her tanks is a gas. "Gas" is also a short word for gasoline, the liquid fuel that makes cars run.

geology (jee-OL-uh-jee) *noun*

Geology is the study of the Earth and what it is made of. People who work in the field of geology are called geologists. Geologists study the history of the Earth, the shapes of the land (such as mountains, domes, and canyons), the different kinds of rocks and minerals, and the causes of earthquakes.

30

geyser (GY-zur) *noun*

A geyser is a natural hole in the ground that spouts steam and hot water into the air. Some geysers spout once every few minutes, and others spout every few months. Old Faithful, in Yellowstone National Park, is a famous geyser that used to spout about every hour but isn't quite so predictable anymore.

Old Faithful

glacier (GLAY-shur) *noun*

A glacier is a field of thick ice that moves very slowly downhill. Glaciers form when snow piles up on a mountainside or along a valley over many years. Most glaciers flow so slowly that you cannot see them moving.

grassland (GRASS-land) *noun*

A grassland is open land covered with grasses. A grassland is too wet to be a desert, but it is also too dry for many trees or shrubs to grow. Most of the grasslands of North America, called prairies, have been turned into farms and pastures, but the ones that are left are full of many different animals, including ground squirrels, hawks, snakes, antelope, and coyotes.

the African grasslands

31

gravity (GRAV-ut-ee) noun

Gravity is a force that pulls things toward each other. It is what makes things fall down, toward the center of a planet or star. Gravity pulls you down a slide. It also keeps you on the Earth, and keeps the Earth near the Sun.

Hh

red-faced cormorants

harbor seal

habitat (HAB-uh-tat) noun

A habitat is a place where a plant or animal normally lives and grows. The Arctic is the habitat of the red-faced cormorant and the harbor seal. The prairie is the bison's habitat. A redwood tree's habitat is coastal forest.

hail (HAYL) noun

Hail is ice that falls from clouds to the ground during storms. The ice falls in little pellets called hailstones. Most hailstones are smaller than your thumbnail, but some hailstones can be bigger than a softball.

heart (HART) *noun*

The heart is the organ that pumps blood—first to the lungs to pick up oxygen and then to the rest of the body. The hearts of humans, and those of many other animals, have hollow chambers that fill up with blood. When the heart muscle contracts, or "beats," blood is squeezed out of the chambers and into the body through tubes called arteries.

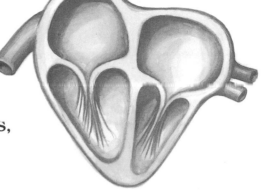

inside view of the heart, showing its chambers

hibernating hamsters

hibernate (HY-bur-nayt) *verb*

During winter, some animals hibernate, or go into a deep sleep. Their bodies become very cold—sometimes almost as cold as ice! Their heartbeat and breathing slow down to conserve energy. When the spring comes, they come out of hibernation until the next winter.

Who really hibernates?

Prairie dogs, marmots, ground squirrels, hamsters, and bats all hibernate. Bears and badgers do sleep deeply in winter, but they do not lower their body temperatures as the other animals do, so they do not truly hibernate.

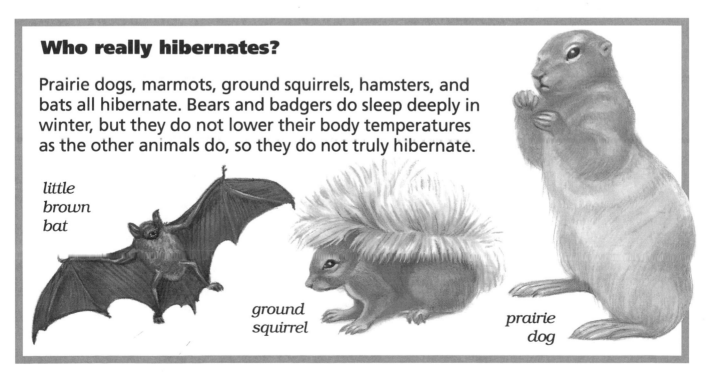

little brown bat

ground squirrel

prairie dog

33

human (HYOO-mun) *noun*

A human, or human being, is a person. All people are humans. The scientific name for a human is *Homo sapiens*, which means "wise or knowing man" in Latin. Humans are very social, ground-dwelling mammals who change the environments in which they live to suit their needs.

humidity (hyoo-MID-ut-ee) *noun*

Humidity is the amount of moisture in the air. On a very humid day, the air feels heavy and damp.

hurricane (HUR-uh-kayn) *noun*

A hurricane is a very strong, tropical storm, with fast, violent, twisting winds and heavy rains. Hurricanes often hit coastal areas. They can destroy boats, buildings, and trees.

Ii

ice (EYSS) *noun*

Ice is frozen water. You know water in three forms: ice (a solid), water (a liquid), and steam (a gas). Water freezes at 32 degrees Fahrenheit and boils, that is becomes a gas, at 212 degrees Fahrenheit.

iceberg (EYSS-burg) *noun*

An iceberg is a large piece of ice floating in a body of water. We see only a small part of an iceberg; most of it is hidden beneath the water's surface. Icebergs can be found in the cold waters toward the North Pole and the South Pole.

insect (IN-sekt) *noun*

An insect is a small, air-breathing animal that typically has three pairs of legs and one or two pairs of wings. Insects have skeletons on the outside of their bodies to protect them like a suit of armor. Female insects lay eggs. Insect bodies are divided into three parts: the head, thorax, and abdomen. Some insects have venomous bites or stings, but many do not. Grasshoppers, cockroaches, bees, and beetles are all insects.

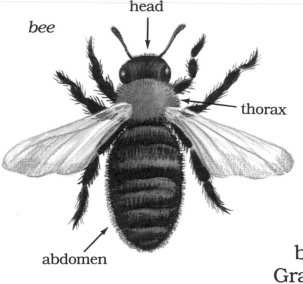

bee

head

thorax

abdomen

More about insects

There are more kinds of insects on Earth than all the other kinds of animals put together. Some insects are so tiny you can hardly see them, and others are as long as this book!

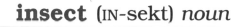

bee

beetle

ant

walking stick

island (EYE-lund) *noun*

An island is a piece of land that is smaller than a continent and totally surrounded by water. You can find islands in oceans, in lakes, and even in rivers and streams. Some islands are formed by underwater volcanoes, like the island of Hawaii.

Jj

jungle (JUN-gul) *noun*. See **rain forest**.

Ll

lake (LAYK) *noun*

A lake is a large pool of water. Lakes are filled by rain, rivers, and streams. Most lakes have fresh water in them, but a few, like the Great Salt Lake in Utah, are salty.

Lake Superior

Isle Royale

landslide (LAND-slyd) *noun*

A landslide is a fast tumble of earth or rock down a hill or mountainside. Landslides happen on steep slopes where the rock is weak or broken, or in places where water has soaked into the ground and made it slippery.

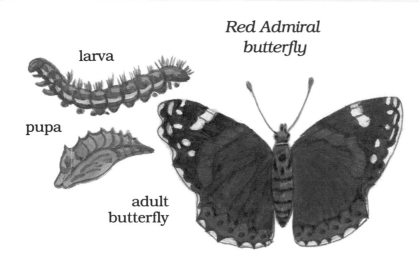

larva

pupa

Red Admiral butterfly

adult butterfly

larva (LAR-vuh) *noun*
plural: larvae (LAR-vee)

A larva is a young animal that looks very different from its parents. When it grows up, a larva changes its shape completely. This change is called metamorphosis (met-uh-MOR-fuh-sis). A caterpillar is the larva of a moth or a butterfly. A tadpole is the larva of a frog.

lava (LAV-uh) *noun*

Lava is the very hot, melted rock that flows out of volcanoes. The word "lava" is also used to describe that same rock after it has cooled and hardened.

aerial view of a volcano

37

leaf (LEEF) *noun*

A leaf is the part of a green plant where most of the plant's food is made. Leaves are usually broad and flat so they can soak up a lot of sunshine. The sunshine gives them the energy needed to make food. Some leaves, like pine needles, are thin and narrow so water within the needles cannot escape.

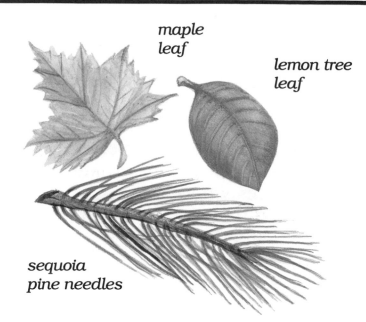

maple leaf

lemon tree leaf

sequoia pine needles

lens (LENZ) *noun*

A lens is a piece of transparent material, such as glass or plastic, that is curved so that it can focus rays of light. Something seen through a lens can seem closer or farther away, sharper or fuzzier, depending on the shape of the lens. The word "lens" comes from "lentil," which is the name of a bean that is shaped like a lens.

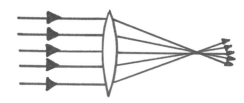

A convex lens brings light waves together.

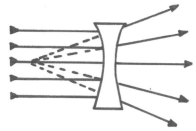

A concave lens spreads light waves apart.

Would you believe . . . ?

Telescopes, magnifying glasses, and cameras all have lenses. And so do you! Each of your eyes has a lens inside it made of clear protein and water. Tiny muscles inside your eye pull on the edges of the lens to change its shape. This lets your eyes focus on things that are close or far away.

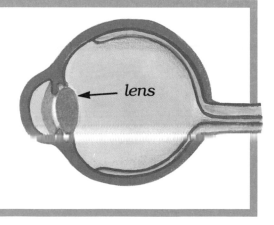

lens

lightning (LYT-ning) *noun*

Lightning is a quick, bright flash of light in the sky. It is caused by a giant electric spark inside a cloud, or between two clouds, or between a cloud and the ground. Lightning is usually shaped like a long, forking, jagged line.

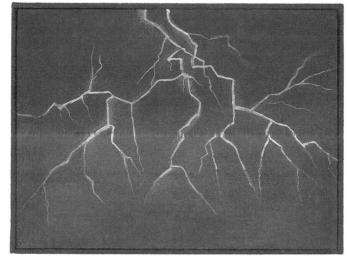

Water is a liquid.

liquid (LIK-wud) *noun, adjective*

Liquid is one of the three states, or forms, that matter comes in. (The other two states are solid and gas.) A liquid is wet and runny, and unlike a gas, it can't be squeezed together to take up less space. A liquid takes the shape of whatever container it is put in. The word "liquid" can also be used to describe something liquid, as in "liquid rock" or "liquid wax."

lunar (LOO-nur) *adjective*

Lunar means having to do with the Moon. A lunar orbit is an orbit around the Moon. A lunar mission is a trip to the Moon.

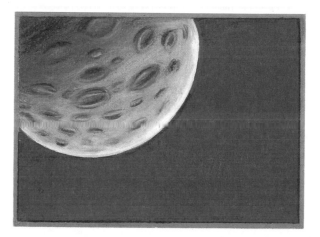

39

lung (LUNG) *noun*

Lungs are organs for breathing air. Many kinds of animals have lungs. Human lungs are spongy and pink and about the size of footballs. There is one lung on each side of your heart.

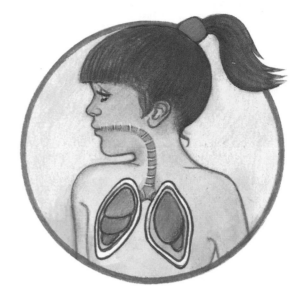

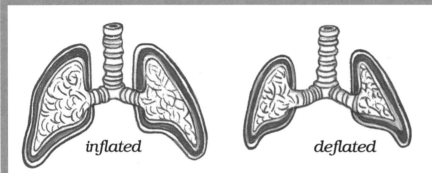

inflated   *deflated*

Your lungs at work

Your lungs fill the space inside your chest from your neck to the bottom of your ribs. When you breathe in, your chest expands and your lungs are filled with fresh air. When you breathe out, the space inside your chest shrinks, and old air is squeezed out of your lungs.

Mm

machine (muh-SHEEN) *noun*

A machine is a tool that can do work. Machines are made of parts that work together. Some of a machine's parts move. Levers and pulleys are two of the simplest machines. Sewing machines and cars are more complicated machines.

pulley

magnet (MAG-net) noun

A magnet is a piece of metal or stone that can attract iron or steel. Magnets can be made by hand, but they can also be found in nature. A horseshoe magnet is made of steel by hand. A lodestone is a natural magnet.

horseshoe magnet

the happy face spider, magnified

magnify (MAG-nuh-fy) verb

To magnify something is to make it look larger. Lenses, as in a telescope or a microscope, can magnify things.

Barbary sheep

mammal (MAM-ul) noun

A mammal is an animal that, when young, is fed by its mother, with milk that she makes in her own body. All mammals have backbones and are warm-blooded, and most mammals are born live and have hair or fur. Humans are mammals. So are mice, cats, whales, and grizzly bears.

marsupial (mar-SOO-pee-ul) *noun*

A marsupial is a kind of mammal that spends the early part of its life inside a skin pouch on its mother's body. Baby marsupials are born small, helpless, and immature. As soon as they are born, they crawl into the mother's pouch, where they live until they are old enough to walk around on their own. Opossums and kangaroos are marsupials.

kangaroo and joey

matter (MAT-ur) *noun*

Everything in the universe that has weight and takes up space is called matter. Matter can be solid, liquid, or gas. Oxygen, dust, water, and stars are made of matter. This book is made of matter, and so are you.

melt (MELT) *verb*

To melt is to be changed from a solid into a liquid by heating. Different things melt at different temperatures. Ice melts in your hand, but it takes the heat of an iron, a flame, or hot sunshine to melt wax crayons.

meteor (MEET-ee-or) *noun*

A meteor is made by a piece of rock or metal that passes through the Earth's atmosphere from outer space at great speed. Friction from rubbing against the air causes the rock to become so hot that it burns and glows as a meteor.

meteor shower

What is a meteroid? A meteorite?

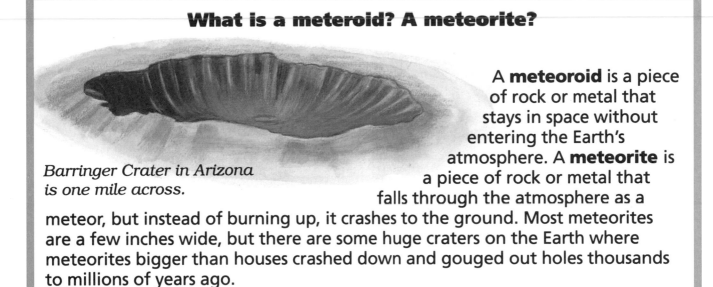

Barringer Crater in Arizona is one mile across.

A **meteoroid** is a piece of rock or metal that stays in space without entering the Earth's atmosphere. A **meteorite** is a piece of rock or metal that falls through the atmosphere as a meteor, but instead of burning up, it crashes to the ground. Most meteorites are a few inches wide, but there are some huge craters on the Earth where meteorites bigger than houses crashed down and gouged out holes thousands to millions of years ago.

microscope
(MY-kruh-skohp) *noun*

A microscope is a tool that uses lenses to make small things look bigger. Magnifying glasses are the simplest microscopes. Fancier microscopes use more than one lens and allow you to see things that are normally invisible, such as a tiny insect that lives on the back of a termite.

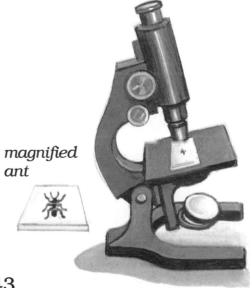
magnified ant

mineral (MIN-uh-rul) noun

Minerals are the ingredients of mountains, rocks, and sand. Most minerals are compounds, which means they are made up of more than one kind of atom. Salt, diamonds, quartz, graphite, and gold are all minerals. Minerals are also found in the foods we eat and in our bodies.

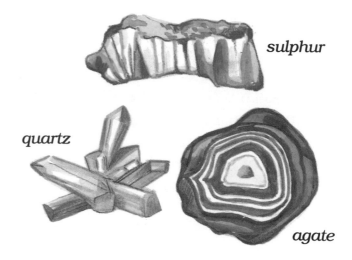

sulphur

quartz

agate

A rose in a glass of water looks bent, but it is only the light bending as it passes from air to water.

mirage (mih-RAZH) noun

A mirage is a kind of optical illusion. It is a mirror image of something like water or a mountain that shows up in a place where there really is no water or mountain. If you think you see a shimmering pool of water on a hot, dry road, it is probably a mirage.

How do mirages happen?

Mirages occur because light bends as it passes between layers of warm air and cool air. This bending light can project an image of something say, a tree or a mountain into a place where there is no tree or mountain. When you see a mirage, you are seeing light that has been bent through layers of warm air and cool air on its way from the tree to you.

monsoon (mon-SOON) noun

A monsoon is a wind that changes direction with the seasons. The most famous monsoons blow in India and Southeast Asia. In summer, these winds are moist and sometimes bring hurricanes. In winter, they are cold and dry.

moon (MOON) noun. See satellite.

regal moth

moth (MOTH) noun

A moth is a kind of insect that has two pairs of wings that work together as a single pair. A moth's wings are covered with tiny, fuzzy scales. Moths have thick, often hairy bodies. They usually feed and fly at night.

biceps muscle

muscle (MUSS-ul) noun

A muscle is a bundle of fibers in your body. There are three types of muscle. One kind enables you to move. Another kind helps with digestion of food and circulation of blood. Your heart is made of the third kind of muscle. It is able to pump blood because it is made of a special kind of muscle.

Nn

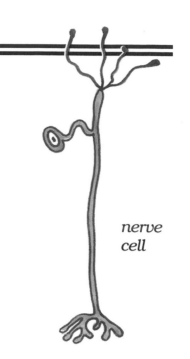

nerve (NERV) *noun*

A nerve is a fiber (or bundle of fibers) in your body. A nerve is made of special cells that send messages from one part of the body to another. These messages give your muscles the signal to contract or relax. The messages also allow you to move, to feel pleasure and pain, and to do just about everything you do.

nerve cell

nutrient (NOO-tree-unt) *noun*

A nutrient is anything that gives nourishment. Food that is good for you is full of nutrients.

Oo

ocean (OH shun) *noun*

The great ocean is the huge body of saltwater that covers almost three-quarters of the Earth's surface. The great ocean is divided into four smaller bodies of water: the Pacific, Atlantic, Indian, and Arctic oceans. Smaller bodies of saltwater are called seas. (See **bay** illustration.)

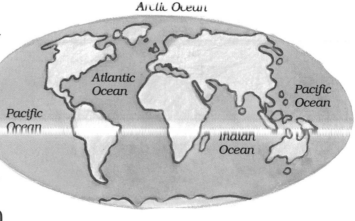

Arctic Ocean

Atlantic Ocean

Pacific Ocean

Pacific Ocean

Indian Ocean

46

orbit (OR-but) *noun, verb*

An orbit is the path an object takes around another object in space. The word "orbit" is also used to mean the action of orbiting: the Earth orbits the Sun.

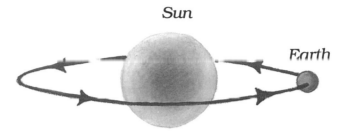

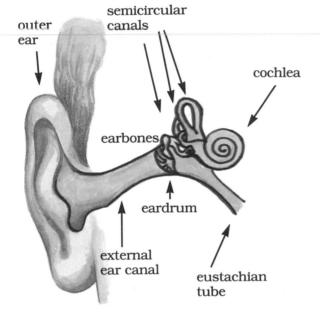

the human ear

organ (OR-gun) *noun*

An organ is a part of an animal, plant, or other organism that has a specific job to do. Hearts, lungs, eyes, and ears are kinds of organs belonging to animals. Leaves, trunks, and stems are kinds of organs belonging to plants.

organism
(OR-guh-niz-um) *noun*

An organism is any living thing. Plants, animals, bacteria, and fungi are all kinds of organisms. You are also an organism.

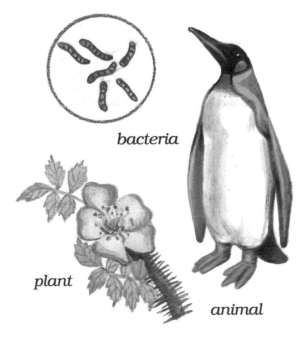

47

oxygen (OK-sih-jun) *noun*

Oxygen is one of the gases in the Earth's atmosphere. Oxygen gas has no color, taste, or smell. Most living things need oxygen to survive.

Pp

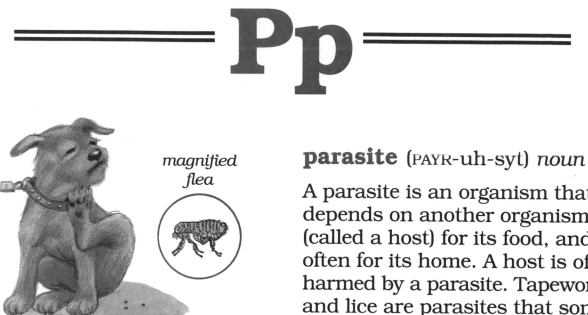

magnified flea

Fleas often use dogs as hosts.

parasite (PAYR-uh-syt) *noun*

A parasite is an organism that depends on another organism (called a host) for its food, and often for its home. A host is often harmed by a parasite. Tapeworms and lice are parasites that some-times use humans as hosts.

planet (PLAN-ut) *noun*

A planet is a body in space that orbits a star, such as the Sun. There are nine planets orbiting our Sun: Mercury, Venus, Earth, Mars, Jupiter, Saturn, Uranus, Neptune, and Pluto.

Jupiter

pollution
(puh-LOO-shun) *noun*

Pollution is contamination of the environment. It is the dirtying of the land, air, or water with harmful substances.

predator
(PRED-ut-ur) *noun*

A predator is an animal that catches, kills, and eats other animals (called prey). Sharks, tigers, and hawks are predators. So are spiders that catch insects in their webs and fungi that capture microscopic animals with the sticky threads that they grow. People can be predators, too.

golden eagle

prey (PRAY) *noun*

Prey is the name given to living things that are caught and eaten by predators.

field mouse

49

Rr

rain (RAYN) *noun*

Rain is a shower of water droplets that fall through the atmosphere from clouds to the ground.

rainbow (RAYN-boh) *noun*

A rainbow is a curving band of colored lights made when sunlight shines on water droplets in the air. You can see a rainbow if you look at mist with the Sun shining behind you. A rainbow's colored stripes are always in the same order: red, orange, yellow, green, blue, indigo, and violet.

rain forest (RAYN FOR-est) *noun*

A rain forest is a thick, tangled growth of trees and other plants that live in a wet place where rain falls throughout the year. Rain forests are home to many different kinds of plants, animals, and other living things. Rain forests in hot, moist places are also called "jungles."

toucan

butterfly

spider

two-toed sloth

50

renewable

(rih-NOO-uh-bul) *adjective*

Something that is renewable can be used again and again without being used up. Solar energy is renewable energy because the Sun's energy does not run out when we use it. Oil and gas are nonrenewable energy sources: they can be used up.

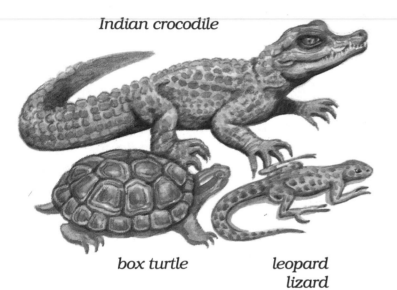

Indian crocodile

box turtle

leopard lizard

reptile (REP-tyl) *noun*

A reptile is a backboned animal that has scaly skin and breathes air through lungs. Most female reptiles lay eggs. A few snakes and lizards have venomous bites, but most reptiles are harmless to people. Snakes, lizards, turtles, tortoises, alligators, and crocodiles are all reptiles.

river (RIV-ur) *noun*

A river is a long ribbon of water that flows downhill into an ocean, a lake, or another river. Rivers can be deep or shallow, wide or narrow, warm or icy, fast or slow. The longest rivers, like the Amazon in South America, are thousands of miles long. (See **bay** illustration.)

river otter

root (ROOT) *noun*

A root is the part of a plant that grows downward into the ground. Roots anchor a plant into the ground and also soak up nutrients and water from the soil. Some roots, like beets and carrots, store food for the plant's use. These roots also make good food for animals.

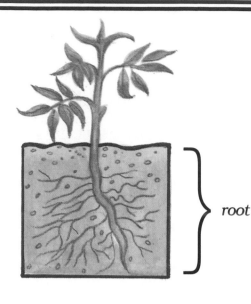

root

satellite (SAT-uh-lyt) *noun*

A satellite is anything that moves in an orbit around a larger object in space. Satellites can be natural or artificial. The Moon is a natural satellite of the Earth. (The natural satellites orbiting many of the other planets in our solar system are also often called moons.) Artificial satellites are machines that have been sent into orbit to take pictures, study the weather, and do other jobs.

Earth

Moon

science (SY-unss) *noun*

Science is the study of the universe, everything in it, and how it all works. Science has many different branches. Biology, geology, astronomy, and chemistry are all branches of science.

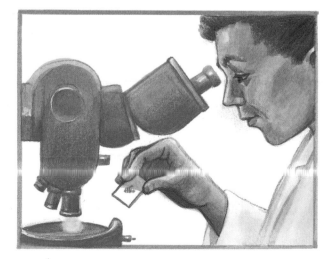

seed (SEED) *noun*

A seed is one way that a plant makes a new plant. A seed is made up of a baby plant that is packed inside a tough coat with a supply of food. All plants that have flowers or cones make seeds. Some seeds are as tiny as dust grains, and some are bigger than coconuts. Coconuts, in fact, are among the biggest of all seeds.

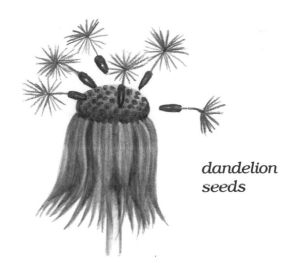

dandelion seeds

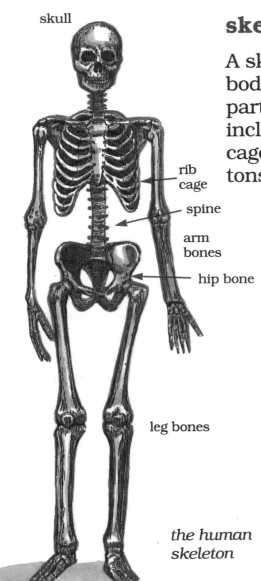

skull

rib cage

spine

arm bones

hip bone

leg bones

the human skeleton

skeleton (SKEL-ut-un) *noun*

A skeleton is the frame of bones that holds up the bodies of certain animals. It also protects the soft parts within these animals' bodies. Your skeleton includes the skull, spine, arm and leg bones, rib cage, and many other bones. Animals with skeletons are called vertebrates (VER-tuh-brayts).

snow (SNOH) *noun*

Snow is made of flakes or clumps of ice crystals that fall through the atmosphere from clouds to the ground. Snow forms when water vapor freezes in very cold air. Snowflakes always have six sides or points, but no two snowflakes are alike.

*the solar system, showing the relative sizes of the planets (above)
and their relative distances from the Sun (below)*

solar system (SOH-lur SISS-tum) *noun*

The solar system is made up of the Sun and all the planets,
moons, asteroids, meteors, comets, gas, and dust that orbit
around it. The term "solar system" comes from the word *sol*,
which means "sun" in Latin.

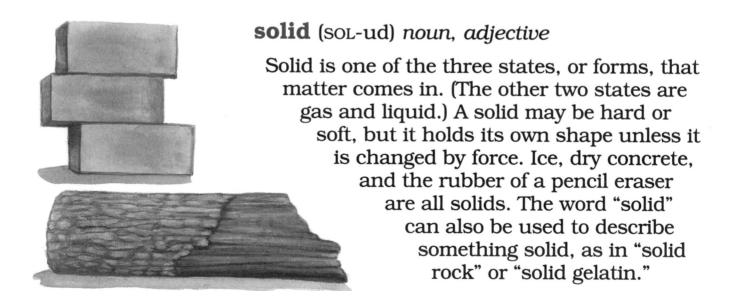

solid (SOL-ud) *noun, adjective*

Solid is one of the three states, or forms, that
matter comes in. (The other two states are
gas and liquid.) A solid may be hard or
soft, but it holds its own shape unless it
is changed by force. Ice, dry concrete,
and the rubber of a pencil eraser
are all solids. The word "solid"
can also be used to describe
something solid, as in "solid
rock" or "solid gelatin."

space (SPAYSS) *noun*

Space (sometimes called "outer space") is everything beyond the
Earth's atmosphere. The word "space" is also used to mean any area
or place: all objects take up space.

sphere (SFEER) *noun*

A sphere is a perfect ball-like shape. Basketballs, globes, and soap bubbles are all spheres.

garden spider

spider (SPYD-ur) *noun*

A spider is a small, air-breathing animal that typically has a two-part body, four pairs of legs, and four pairs of eyes. Spiders have skeletons on the outside of their bodies. They make silk thread for weaving webs and cocoons, tying up prey, or spinning out lines that let them float and dangle. Spiders paralyze their prey with venom. Spiders are related to scorpions and ticks.

star (STAR) *noun*

A star is a giant ball of very hot glowing gas in space. The Sun is the star nearest to Earth. All other stars are so far away that they look like tiny points of light in our sky, even though most that you see are larger than our Sun. The universe contains trillions of stars.

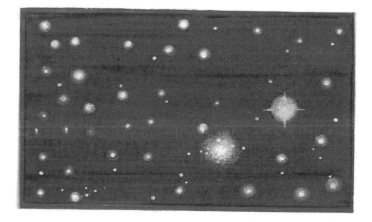

Tt

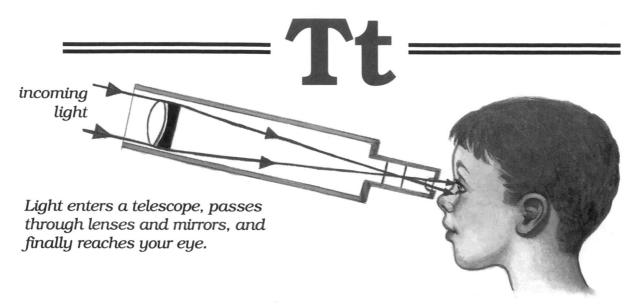

incoming light

Light enters a telescope, passes through lenses and mirrors, and finally reaches your eye.

telescope (TEL-uh-skohp) *noun*

A telescope is a tool for seeing things that are very faint or very far away. Telescopes are made with lenses and mirrors, which can gather more light than our eyes can. Telescopes make objects appear nearer and larger than they normally do.

temperature
(TEM-per-chur) *noun*

Temperature tells you how hot or how cold something is. Temperature is measured in degrees (°). The normal temperature of a human body is between 97°F and 99°F. Water freezes at 32°F. The "F" stands for Fahrenheit, the name of the man who invented a way of measuring temperature.

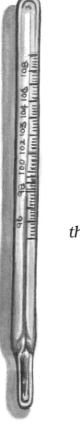

thermometer

thermometer
(ther-MOM-ut-ur) *noun*

A thermometer measures temperature. The most common kind of thermometer is a glass tube that is partly filled with a liquid metal called mercury. When the mercury warms up, it expands and rises up the tube.

thunder (THUN-dur) noun

Thunder is a loud crack or rumble in the air during a storm. Thunder is caused by lightning. The hot spark of a lightning flash heats up the air, which sends a loud sound wave thundering through the air.

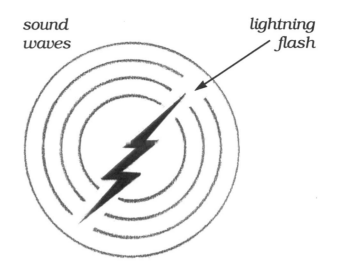

sound waves

lightning flash

low tide

high tide

tide (TYD) noun

The tides are the daily rise and fall of the ocean's surface. They are caused by the pull of both the Moon and Sun's gravity on the Earth. You can see the rise and fall of the tides at the seashore.

tornado (tor-NAYD-oh) noun

A tornado is a very violent, funnel-shaped whirling wind that reaches down to the ground from a storm cloud. Tornadoes occur all over the world, but in certain areas they occur rather frequently. One such place is Tornado Alley in the midwestern United States.

tundra (TUN-druh) *noun*

Tundra is open land where it is too cold and too wet for large plants such as trees to grow. However, smaller plants such as mosses, shrubs, and flowers can grow. In the Arctic tundra, near the North Pole, the ground just under the top layer of soil is permanently frozen. Tundra is also found on high mountains throughout the world.

polar bear

Uu

universe
(YOO-nuh-vurss) *noun*

The universe is everything that exists and happens everywhere.

Vv

vapor (VAY-pur) *noun.* See **gas.**

vein (VAYN) *noun*

Veins are the long, bluish, flexible tubes (also called blood vessels) that return blood from all parts of the body to your heart. If you look at the skin of your wrists or ankles, you may be able to see some veins.

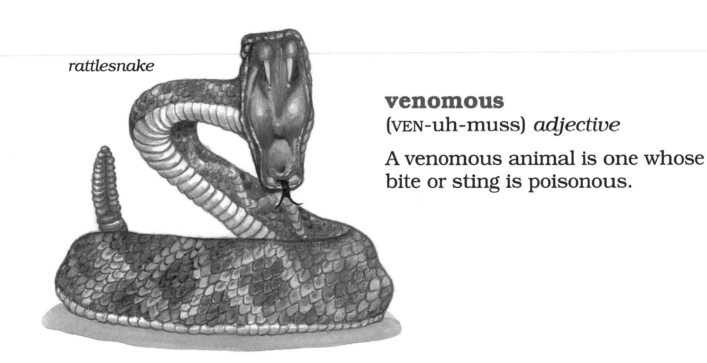

rattlesnake

venomous

(VEN-uh-muss) *adjective*

A venomous animal is one whose bite or sting is poisonous.

virus (VY-russ) *noun*

A virus is a tiny organism that is much smaller than a cell. Viruses cannot live on their own. They must infect the cells of other organisms, such as animals, plants, fungi, or bacteria. They use the infected cells to make more viruses. Just as there are many kinds of plants and animals, there are many kinds of viruses.

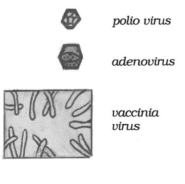

polio virus

adenovirus

vaccinia virus

magnified viruses

59

volcano (vol-KAY-noh) *noun*

A volcano is a crack or hole in the Earth's crust, through which steam, ashes, and hot liquid rock sometimes erupt or flow out from deep inside the Earth. The liquid rock, called lava, sometimes comes out in a big explosion. It then cools, hardens, and forms a cone-shaped mountain, which is also called a volcano.

cross section of an erupting volcano

Ww

The humpback whale and the human diver are both warm-blooded.

warm-blooded (WARM BLUD-ed) *adjective*

Warm-blooded animals are animals whose body temperatures remain constant even when the temperature of their surroundings changes. Mammals and birds are warm-blooded. Scientists think that some extinct dinosaurs were also warm-blooded.

weed (WEED) *noun*

dandelion

A weed is any plant that grows where people do not want it to grow. Weeds compete with more desirable plants for water, light, and room to grow.

Yy

yeast (YEEST) *noun*

Yeast is the name of tiny round fungi that are so small you need a microscope to see them. Some yeasts cause diseases, while others are used in making food, beer, and wine.

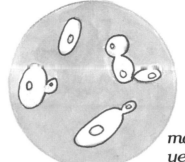

magnified yeast fungi

Why do we use yeast to make bread?

People often use yeast to make bread. When the yeast is added to water, flour, and sugar, it eats the sugar and gives off bubbles of carbon dioxide. The bubbles make the bread dough rise, which in turn makes the bread light and fluffy when it is baked.

Zz

zoology (zoh-OL-uh-jee) *noun*

Zoology is the study of animals: their body shapes, growth and development, behavior, and grouping into different categories. People who work in the field of zoology are called zoologists.

hatching crocodile